Some Mornings

Other Poetry Books By Nelson Ball

You Must Look Hard To See What's There (press-press-pull, 2014)
Three-Letter Words (2nd edition, press-press-pull, 2014)
A Rattle Of Spring Frogs (Hamilton Arts & Letters, 2014, online)
Minutiae (Apt. 9 Press, 2014)
A Gathering (new edition, BookThug, 2014)
Orphans (Rubblestone Press, 2012)
The Continuous Present (Proper Tales Press, 2012)
In This Thin Rain (Mansfield Press, 2012)
Nine Poems (Rubblestone Press, 2011)
Three-Letter Words (Laurel Reed Books, 2006)
At The Edge Of The Frog Pond (The Mercury Press, 2004)
With Held (Laurel Reed Books, 2004)
Scrub Cedar (above/ground press, 2003)
A Gathering (Rubblestone Press, 2003)
Almost Spring (The Mercury Press, 1999)
Visitation (Rubblestone Press, 1998)
To Share That Yellow (fingerprinting inkoperated, 1998)
The Concrete Air (The Mercury Press, 1996)
Round Table (Letters, 1996)
Small Gardens (fingerprinting inkoperated, 1996)
Bird Tracks On Hard Snow (ECW Press, 1994)
Fifteen Poems (MindWare, 1994)
Sightings (Curvd H&z, 1992)
With Issa: Poems 1964-1971 (ECW Press, 1991)
Force Movements (2nd edition, Curvd H&z, 1990)
Round Stone (Weed/Flower Press, 1971)
Points Of Attention (Weed/Flower Press, 1971)
The Pre-Linguistic Heights (Coach House Press, 1970)
Water-Pipes And Moonlight (Weed/Flower Press, 1969)
Force Movements (Ganglia Press, 1969)
Sparrows (Weed/Flower Press, 1968)
Beaufort's Scale (Weed/Flower Press, 1967)
Room Of Clocks (Weed/Flower Press, 1965)

Books Edited

Konfessions Of An Elizabethan Fan Dancer by bpNichol (Coach House Books, 2004)
Frank Harrington's Kristmiss Book (The Mercury Press, 1993)

Some Mornings

Nelson Ball

Mansfield Press

a stuart ross book

Printed in Canada

Library and Archives Canada Cataloguing in Publication

Ball, Nelson, 1942-, author
Some mornings / Nelson Ball.

Poems.
ISBN 978-1-77126-057-2 (pbk.)

I. Title.

PS8503.A59S64 2014 C811'.54 C2014-905715-6

Editor for the press: Stuart Ross
Cover design: Denis De Klerck
Cover image: Shutterstock
Typesetting: Stuart Ross
Author photo: Catherine Stevenson

The publication of *Some Mornings* has been generously supported by the Canada Council for the Arts and the Ontario Arts Council.

Canada Council for the Arts / Conseil des Arts du Canada

ONTARIO ARTS COUNCIL
CONSEIL DES ARTS DE L'ONTARIO

Mansfield Press Inc.
25 Mansfield Avenue, Toronto, Ontario, Canada M6J 2A9
Publisher: Denis De Klerck
www.mansfieldpress.net

In memory of my soulmate, Barbara Caruso

Contents

Some Mornings

Some mornings
as I awaken

I compose a poem
in my head

usually gone
when I get to my desk

this morning
I caught one

Writing Surface

For John Riddell and derek beaulieu
and Lori Emerson

Stubs
of pale corn stalks

point
every whichway

on the dark
ploughed

earth's
new face

Signs: January (Temperature 0; Windy)

Falling
snow

moves
horizontally

sticking
to

trees
rooves

poles
fences

filling
the gaps

in every
thing

Signs: February

For Trisha Little

Snow
rises in air

above
the fields

revealing
the secret animation

of
the wind

A Rattle Of Spring Frogs

When
they are close

they sound
like a two-stroke engine in the distance —

a motorcycle, or
a chainsaw —

but no
it's frogs

the rattle
of frogs

Late Fall

Dried, brown, curled
the small leaves

skitter about
on the paved road

frenzied animals
looking for escape

Talk

To Barbara in absentia

Barbara
you talked a lot

now
you are gone

you
continue

speaking
to me

but not
nearly enough

A Moment

Frost
glistens
the glass

tears
glisten
her eyes

Jack Pine

Like a painting
of itself

in wide
short

brush
strokes

its
smooth

grey
bark

turns
dark

and
scaly

In Winter

At the fruit farm
the bare trees

look
like

startled
octopi

Landscape

Veils
of rain

pale
grey

obscure
detail

make
strange

Yellow

In rural southwestern Ontario
whole fields of yellow

in spring of dandelions
goldenrod in the fall

Sensory Perception

For Catherine and her kids, Lucas and Owen

I wrote a birthday greeting to my friend Catherine
on notecard Barbara had made

a reproduction of her ink drawing
involving patterns of straight lines

When Catherine showed it to little Owen
he gently ran his hand across the image

to feel the texture
of what he saw

What?

For and after Patrick Campbell

My friend Patrick is skeptical
about corporations calling their products green

We were at the garage, Patrick
advising me in the choice of summer tires

when the dealer pointed to a poster and said
"Those are a new product, and they're green."

"What," Patrick muttered under his breath,
"made of tofu?"

My Caffeine

In the morning
I listen to “Lover Come Back To Me”

with Yukiko Onishi
on sax

and Senri
Kawaguchi

the young drummer
who drums

like a machine
gunner

drumming
my sleep away

Side Streets

At Mount Pleasant
in rural Ontario

the side streets end
at the edges of cornfields

April 16, 2012: Visible Air

For Anita Campbell

A mild day
sun and cloud

strong
winds

air dulled
by fine soil

rising
from tilled fields

except here
and there

it's as thick
as smoke

Vantage Point

From
the open field

the dense
woodlot

appears
without light

dark
as a cave

A Form Of Grief

In memory of Barbara
and our friend bpNichol

Barbara and I
when we learned

of the death
of our friend

engaged in passionate
prolonged lovemaking

desperately
clinging to each other

asserting life
clinging to it

Shifting Stitches

Geese

high

in the grey sky

Reversion

The Kindy Air Field
near Rainham Centre

is now put
in beans

A Hawk

teeters and tips
in a holding pattern

forty feet
above the field

Unheard

I infer
trains are crossing the iron bridge tonight

but I can’t
hear them —

the noise of the high wind
against the house

drowns out
all other sound

An Unstated Question

Corn
growing near the cemetery

is very
tall

The Squirrel

As I walked by
a dead squirrel

the fur of its tail lifted
in a momentary breeze

then fell back
dead still

Yikes!

Too many of the people
in my address book

are dead, and too many others
I don't remember

Pure Energy

Rapid
frantic

wings
flutter

the young bird
mislands

on
the
wire

seeks

footing

Of Bopp And Ice And Rock

Thomas Bopp
is an amateur astronomer

co-discoverer
of the Hale-Bopp comet

not
a musician

not
related to Bill Haley

Pissing On An Electric Fence

The main text of this poem
as yet unwritten

is likely
to remain so

with
good aim

and
luck

Furtively

When I write a word with two adjacent e's
they become a pair of eyes

watching
me

You Must Look Hard To See What's There

In memory of David UU [David W. Harris]

He read
a poetry manuscript

several
times

at different
times of day

in different
locations

David UU
told me

that's
what he did

now
that's what I do

Quietude

High in the still air
        the turkey vulture
                gently works its wings

Note

The tip
of the yew bough

dips

in fits
and
starts

in the recurrent
wind

Birds

A mourning dove
asserts its ancient right

builds a nest
in the tree near my door

It gathers twigs
most too large for use

and drops those
on the sidewalk below

where I
step around

twigs
and poop

It's Spring!

For M.R. (Rob) Appell

Loud
inside the house

sometimes
a thud

sometimes
bang and rattle

a
bird

driven
by

unstoppable
lust

strikes
a window

Longevity Assured

cement

fence

posts

Landscape

Clouds' shadows
          wander
                    on the land

Form

Stalwart hickory
holds its form
while the cedar bends in the wind

Authenticity

A new headstone
at the cemetery

awaits certification
by birds

Question

Why
does

that
twig

wiggle?

The Monster (Carp) In The Pond

Straight
up

sudden
leap

then the
fall

back
with

whack
and

splash
!!!

Bookstore Enquiry

"How do you clean your books?"

"What do you mean?"

"How do you get rid of the germs?"

To Bernadette Rule And Her Lovely Daughter, Caris

At Green Heron Books, April 14, 2013

We were gathering for a reading
by Janet Hepburn, launching her novel

about two seniors on the lam
from their nursing home

and for readings from an anthology guided by Bernadette Rule
of fictional memoirs of forgotten women

when a pretty young girl sat down
one row in front of me:

A mirage
I thought

a
nymphet

where
am I?

After The Refugee Camp

For the unadulterated luxury
of plentitude, little Pam

puts ketchup
on her chocolate cake

One Way, Then Another

Black night sky
        turns blue
                in the lightning's light

In the night sky
        lightning's light blue
                turns black

New Etiquette

Older farmhouses —
front steps

removed
when the wood rotted —

testify
to changed etiquette

Now everyone
enters by the side door

even the pastor
and the insurance salesman

The Mouse

Occasionally
I catch a mouse

on my trapline
in the basement

once
I found a mouse

dead
in a trap

and lying
close by

untouched
by the trap

another
dead mouse

it nearly
broke my heart

when
I told Barbara

her eyes
filled with tears

Dense

fog's
a merger

of grounds

at
the fore

September Breeze

I watched
a baby turtle

cross the gravel road
moving more slowly

than a curled leaf
in the slight breeze

Point Of View

Beside
the Rail Trail

lies
a red woolen glove

it's lain
there

for
weeks

the other
glove

is
lost

Poop On A Picnic Table

For Kate Belair, at the Homestead

I am mentioned again on the Facebook page
of the Adelaide Hunter Hoodless Homestead

"Where's our resident poet
... when we need him"

in the context of the discovery by Clayton Barker
of mysterious poop on a picnic table

that I wasn't there to see
and write a poem about

It is nice to know
someone thought of me

when I wasn't there, even
in the context of poop

Geese

While their wings flap slowly
they move forward

like
rockets

waving
goodbye

The New Decorum

In this region
near the Great Lakes

one occasionally sees
in the driveway

of a tidy house, a boat
as big as the house

sometimes
it's on the lawn

a middle-class thing
the new decorum

Blue Devil In January

Among
the grasses'

browns
and greys

a hint
of blue

Driving

A road
in dense fog

seems
longer

so much
longer

almost
endless

Autumn

Gunmetal sky
        of greying September
                above a field of restless corn

On the road
        I steer around
                a skittering leaf

Animated in wind
        the spruce branches move
                like waves on the lake

Diets

For Liz Ball and Pat Moore

Lambs
eat ivy

moose
eat water lilies

horses
eat shrubs

man
eats lamb

and
moose

sometimes
horse

peculiar
eh?

At The Ponds

For Kemeny Babineau and Laurie Dunn

Anomaly

A small
translucent fish

swims
in shallow water

above
its darker shadow

Map In Motion

Moss-like islands
float freely within

a large area of duckweed —
the surface film whereon

these moving islands
map themselves

Precarious

A tiny island
of floating plant debris

moss-like, flimsy
barely larger

than the young turtle
sunning itself

Resilient

Separated
from a shoreline shrub

a thin branch
floats among the detritus

shows three
new green sprouts

pointing
skyward

Fred And The Ladder

Hilda asked
"Why is the ladder still out?"

Fred didn't remember
so he put it away

in the driving shed
where it belongs

having left it out
for months, leaning

against the edge
of the roof

Catherine: Moving House: April 30, 2013

To my friend Catherine Stevenson

On the final day of your move to Waterford
the house you were leaving in Paris
was not empty

In four hours the ownership would
transfer and there was
much remaining

Your friend Suzan deftly packed food
and other things, in boxes,
and swept the floor

I carried light things and packed my car
then took light things to your car
you carried the heavy stuff

But for just a few minutes
you sat on the floor
and sorted coat hangers

I watched you gathering yourself
resting, recovering, and, perhaps,
mourning this home

Anomaly

At the centre
of a vast paved parking lot

for Staples, Food Basics,
Canadian Tire and others

where there is no
visible living thing

an odour
of skunk

Dead Men

For Jim Bechtel

We name things
the short tree beyond the field

for its shape
"dead man standing"

the projection of shore
where the ice fisherman's

body was found
"dead man's point"

Jim says, "We take the days
one at a time"

we know
what comes next

Conflation

At Delhi
in rural Ontario

there is a long gap
between two houses along a main street

where a tobacco field
joins the town

Conversion

In the bay
of Baie du Doré

where water levels
have receded

are new
islands

of long grass
and short trees

E-Mail Enquiry

"Do you have a book by William Guy Carr
titled *Games in the Pond*?"

Sixteen minutes later
a second e-mail:

"Sorry, the name of the book
is *Pawns in the Game.*"

Little Things (Mean A Lot)

To Mary Neff, in memory of Nelson Neff

In the pocket
of his favourite golf jacket

three candy wrappers
and a shopping list:

coffee
coffee cream

lettuce
hamburger

bread
shaving cream

ice cream —

his
minutiae

Calista

Calista Counter
lived in Clinton

across
the street

when I
was five

I wished
I had a sister

named
Calista

Br(eye)an David Johnston

For Linda Besner and Leigh Kotsilidis

He's going to read
his poems for the FishQuillPoetryBoat landing
at Paris on June 20th.

He says it takes
eight minutes to read his poems. So he also
will read some of mine.

I suggest he not read longer
than ten minutes. He says
"Good, I'll pick just the gems

then everyone will think
we write only gems."

A Monument

Robert cut firewood for the stove
and stacked it at a corner of the woodlot.

Then he died. Mabel sold the place
and moved into town. That was four years ago.

The well-stacked wood remains in place
unused, a reminder, almost a monument.

Catherine

Does Catherine collect little boys?
She has two real ones

Owen, age six
Lucas, age ten

I suspect her friend Clayton, age 50
is a little boy

I am
at age 71

At The Farmhouse

When the wind rises
do the little kids wait

expectantly
at the windows

for the old barn
to fall down?

Anomaly

Riding
on rising air

with ease and grace
the turkey vulture

an elegant
scavenger

glides
and slides

Ahead

In the distance
on a roadside hill

either
tree stumps

or
gravestones

East Of Plattsville

On the regional highway east of Plattsville
is a metal fabricating plant

it used to be
a pickle factory

every time I drive past now
coming from either direction

my eyes well up
as I think of Barbara

this happens
every time

always
unexpected

until
now

Notes And Acknowledgements

Barbara was the first reader of my poems and I was the first viewer of her paintings and drawings and first reader of her writings. One afternoon while Barbara was in palliative care and experiencing aphasia, I said to her, "We were a good team." She looked at me and said very firmly, "We *are* a good team." I miss her.

I further dedicate this book to my sisters Elizabeth Ball and Mary Neff and to friends, among them Cameron Anstee, Kemeny Babineau, Clayton Barker, Kate Belair, Anita Campbell, Patrick Campbell, Kathryn Carter, Larry Cowan, Laurie Dunn, Brian David Johnston, Trisha Little, Patricia Moore, Jackie Morris, Tomoko Okumura, Stuart Ross, Catherine Stevenson (and her kids Owen and Lucas), Bob Tees, Sheila Vollmer and Suzan Yates.

Barbara's eyes brightened when Tomoko Okumura and Bob Tees played and sang at her bedside in palliative care. She smiled when Tomoko sang in Japanese. The window view from Barbara's bed was solely of the sky. Bob asked if she wanted to write a song with him. She did. His song incorporates words and phrases she spoke to him in this cooperative effort. The song is called "A Canvas Of Sky," and it makes me cry.

I'm deeply grateful to Anita Campbell who read drafts of all the poems. Her insights, questions and suggestions were invaluable. I'm grateful to Kemeny Babineau for his astute comments and suggestions. To Stuart Ross for suggesting seemingly slight word changes that are astonishing in their effectiveness. Larry Cowan told me which poems he liked best. Catherine Stevenson's comments on several poems were very helpful. Thanks to all of you.

I'm honoured that Stuart selected these poems for "a stuart ross book" and grateful to Denis De Klerck for publishing it. Thanks to you both.

"At The Ponds"
The ponds are located at the Nature Park in the town of Mount Pleasant, Ontario, where Kemeny Babineau, Laurie Dunn and their daughters Aisha and Calantha reside. There are three ponds there that in the early 20th century were part of the first provincial fish hatchery.

"Blue Devil In January"
Blue devil (*Echium vulgare*), also known as viper's bugloss and blue weed, inhabits the meadow west of Green Lane (on the outskirts of the town of Paris), where it colours the field. The name Green Lane relates to agricultural fertilizer produced in Paris in the 19th century from mined gypsum.

"Br(eye)an David Johnston"
The FishQuillPoetryBoat is an annual event that took place on the Grand River in southwestern Ontario 2010–2013. It was organized by Linda Besner and Leigh Kotsilidis, who each year gathered several poets and a musician. Together they paddled down the Grand, stopping to give poetry readings and musical performances. Local poets and musicians were invited to participate at each stop.

"Conversion"
Baie du Doré is on Lake Huron north of Kincardine, Ontario.

"Longevity Assured"
I found cement fence posts in Huron County.

"The Monster (Carp) In The Pond" and "A Rattle Of Spring Frogs"
The carp and frogs inhabit the Nature Park in Mount Pleasant.

"The Mouse"
This is a true story.

"Poop On A Picnic Table"
The Adelaide Hunter Hoodless Homestead is situated near St. George, Ontario. It is a National Historic Site. The spacious grounds include a variety of trees and an open-air picnic pavilion. It is an area where I frequently went for walks after Barbara died. The sole building is the restored farmhouse where Adelaide Hunter (1858–1910) grew up. She married John Hoodless in 1881 and thereafter lived with him in Hamilton. The building houses a museum of the domestic life of her time and honours her accomplishments. Adelaide Hoodless was a tireless promoter of a better and safer life for rural women and children through her many efforts, including cofounding the Women's Institutes, instigating the teaching of domestic science in schools and cofounding the National Council of Women. She is one of Canada's greatest pioneer women but is not widely known. Through friendship with the Museum Curator, Catherine Stevenson, whom I met during one of my walks, I became an occasional volunteer, particularly at two events in 2013 — John Bray Day and the Summer Fête. John Bray was a veteran of the War of 1812 who settled here, built the first farmhouse, and lived here until 1852 when the property was sold to David Hunter, Adelaide's father. The irrepressible Kate Belair was on staff as the Volunteer Development Coordinator. More recently, Kate has become Co-Curator of the Museum and Executive Director of the Federated Women's Institutes of Canada, the National Office of which is located at the Homestead. Clayton Barker is a consultant on the architectural history of the Homestead.

"To Bernadette Rule And Her Lovely Daughter, Caris"
The books referred to are *Flee, Fly, Flown* by Janet Hepburn, Second Story Press, 2013, and *In The Wings: Stories of Forgotten Women*, edited by Bernadette Rule, Seraphim, 2012.

"An Unstated Question"
The cemetery is Baird's Presbyterian Cemetery, near Varna, Ontario.

"Writing Surface"
The title, and to some extent the imagery, are in reference to John Riddell's book *Writing Surfaces: Selected Fiction*, edited and introduced by derek beaulieu and Lori Emerson, Wilfrid Laurier University Press, 2013.

"You Must Look Hard To See What's There"
The title bounces off the title of Donato Mancini's book *You Must Work Harder To Write Poetry Of Excellence*, BookThug, 2012, a critical examination of the conservative nature of reviews since 1961 of books of innovative Canadian poetry.

Some of the poems were published in a chapbook titled *Minutiae*, from Cameron Anstee's Apt. 9 Press; in *You Must Look Hard To See What's There*, a chapbook published by Jim Clinefelter in Portland, Oregon, under his press-press-pull imprint; in *A Rattle Of Spring Frogs*, an online chapbook with a foreword and an essay by R. Bruce Elder on the website *Hamilton Arts & Letters*, edited and published by Paul Lisson and Fiona Kinsella; in the anthology *Fish Quill Poetry Boat 2010–2013*, assembled by Linda Besner and Leigh Kotsilidis; in the poetry magazines *Stone The Crows!*, edited by Larry Cowan, and *Illiterature*, edited by Michael e. Casteels. Thanks to all of you. Several poems were circulated privately as leaflets under my Rubblestone Press imprint.

The poems were written in 2013.

Thanks to the Ontario Arts Council for a Writers' Reserve grant in 2013.

Nelson Ball
May 2014

Nelson Ball is a poet and bookseller living in Paris, Ontario. He has worked as a labourer, chauffeur, clerk, seasonal forest ranger, record store clerk, and janitor. From 1965 to 1973 he ran the legendary Weed/Flower Press, publishing mimeo editions of early books by Victor Coleman, Carol Bergé, David McFadden, bill bissett, bpNichol, and many others. He is the author of 30 poetry books and chapbooks.

Other Books From Mansfield Press

Poetry

Leanne Averbach, *Fever*
Nelson Ball, *In This Thin Rain*
Gary Barwin, *Moon Baboon Canoe*
George Bowering, *Teeth: Poems 2006–2011*
Stephen Brockwell, *Complete Surprising Fragments of Improbable Books*
Stephen Brockwell & Stuart Ross, eds., *Rogue Stimulus: The Stephen Harper Holiday Anthology for a Prorogued Parliament*
Diana Fitzgerald Bryden, *Learning Russian*
Alice Burdick, *Flutter*
Alice Burdick, *Holler*
Jason Camlot, *What The World Said*
Margaret Christakos, *wipe.under.a.love*
Pino Coluccio, *First Comes Love*
Marie-Ève Comtois, *My Planet of Kites*
Dani Couture, *YAW*
Gary Michael Dault, *The Milk of Birds*
Frank Davey, *Poems Suitable for Current Material Conditions*
Pier Giorgio Di Cicco, *The Dark Time of Angels*
Pier Giorgio Di Cicco, *Dead Men of the Fifties*
Pier Giorgio Di Cicco, *The Honeymoon Wilderness*
Pier Giorgio Di Cicco, *Living in Paradise*
Pier Giorgio Di Cicco, *Early Works*
Pier Giorgio Di Cicco, *The Visible World*
Salvatore Difalco, *What Happens at Canals*
Christopher Doda, *Aesthetics Lesson*
Christopher Doda, *Among Ruins*
Glenn Downie, *Monkey Soap*
Rishma Dunlop, *The Body of My Garden*
Rishma Dunlop, *Lover Through Departure: New and Selected Poems*
Rishma Dunlop, *Metropolis*
Rishma Dunlop & Priscila Uppal, eds., *Red Silk: An Anthology of South Asian Women Poets*
Ollivier Dyens, *The Profane Earth*
Laura Farina, *Some Talk of Being Human*
Jaime Forsythe, *Sympathy Loophole*
Carole Glasser Langille, *Late in a Slow Time*
Suzanne Hancock, *Another Name for Bridge*
Jason Heroux, *Emergency Hallelujah*
Jason Heroux, *Memoirs of an Alias*
Jason Heroux, *Natural Capital*
John B. Lee, *In the Terrible Weather of Guns*
Jeanette Lynes, *The Aging Cheerleader's Alphabet*
David W. McFadden, *Be Calm, Honey*
David W. McFadden, *Shouting Your Name Down the Well: Tankas and Haiku*
David W. McFadden, *What's the Score?*
Leigh Nash, *Goodbye, Ukulele*
Lillian Necakov, *The Bone Broker*
Lillian Necakov, *Hooligans*
Peter Norman, *At the Gates of the Theme Park*
Peter Norman, *Water Damage*
Natasha Nuhanovic, *Stray Dog Embassy*
Catherine Owen & Joe Rosenblatt, with Karen Moe, *Dog*
Corrado Paina, *The Alphabet of the Traveler*
Corrado Paina, *The Dowry of Education*
Corrado Paina, *Hoarse Legend*
Corrado Paina, *Souls in Plain Clothes*
Stuart Ross et al., *Our Days in Vaudeville*
Matt Santateresa, *A Beggar's Loom*
Matt Santateresa, *Icarus Redux*
Ann Shin, *The Last Thing Standing*
Jim Smith, *Back Off, Assassin! New and Selected Poems*
Jim Smith, *Happy Birthday, Nicanor Parra*
Robert Earl Stewart, *Campfire Radio Rhapsody*
Robert Earl Stewart, *Something Burned on the Southern Border*
Carey Toane, *The Crystal Palace*
Priscila Uppal, *Summer Sport: Poems*
Priscila Uppal, *Winter Sport: Poems*
Steve Venright, *Floors of Enduring Beauty*
Brian Wickers, *Stations of the Lost*

Fiction

Marianne Apostolides, *The Lucky Child*
Sarah Dearing, *The Art of Sufficient Conclusions*
Denis De Klerck, ed., *Particle & Wave: A Mansfield Omnibus of Electro-Magnetic Fiction*
Paula Eisenstein, *Flip Turn*
Sara Heinonen, *Dear Leaves, I Miss You All*
Christine Miscione, *Carafola*
Marko Sijan, *Mongrel*
Tom Walmsley, *Dog Eat Rat*

Non-Fiction

George Bowering, *How I Wrote Certain of My Books*
Rosanna Cairra & Tony Aspler, *Buon Appetito Toronto*
Denis De Klerck & Corrado Paina, eds., *College Street–Little Italy: Toronto's Renaissance Strip*
Pier Giorgio Di Cicco, *Municipal Mind: Manifestos for the Creative City*
Amy Lavender Harris, *Imagining Toronto*
David W. McFadden, *Mother Died Last Summer*

For a complete list of Mansfield Press titles, please visit mansfieldpress.net